W9-AMQ-620

Are You Living?

A Song About Living and Nonliving Things

by Laura Purdie Salas

illustrated by Viviana Garofoli

Science Songs

Sing along to the tune of

"Are You Sleeping?"

Learn the difference between things that are living and things that are not.

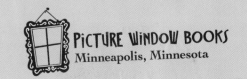

PICTURE WINDOW BOOKS
Minneapolis, Minnesota

Editor: Jill Kalz
Designer: Abbey Fitzgerald
Page Production: Melissa Kes
Art Director: Nathan Gassman
Editorial Director: Nick Healy
The illustrations in this book were created digitally.

Picture Window Books
151 Good Counsel Drive
P.O. Box 669
Mankato, MN 56002-0669
877-845-8392
www.picturewindowbooks.com

Printed in the United States of America.

Library of Congress Cataloging-in-Publication Data
Salas, Laura Purdie.
Are you living? : a song about living and nonliving things /
by Laura Purdie Salas ; illustrated by Viviana Garofoli.
p. cm. – (Science Songs)
Includes index.
ISBN 978-1-4048-5302-7 (library binding)
1. Life (Biology)–Juvenile literature. I. Garofoli, Viviana, ill. II. Title.
QH309.2.S25 2009
570–dc22   2008037915

Thanks to our advisers for their expertise, research, and advice:

Virg Debban, Secondary Science Teacher (ret.)
New Ulm (Minnesota) Public School ISD #88

Terry Flaherty, Ph.D., Professor of English
Minnesota State University, Mankato

Look at the things around you. Some are living. Others are nonliving. Some nonliving things, such as rocks and water, are made by nature. Other nonliving things, such as buildings and books, are made by people.

Watch something. Does it move? Does it grow? Can it make more of itself? Your answers will tell you if the thing is living. If the answer to all three questions is yes, it is alive.

Living things have certain needs. All living beings need air, water, food, and a place to live. Plants also need sunlight. Without it, they will die.

Are you living?

Are you living?

Do you eat?

Do you sleep?

4

If you need to breathe air,

Move from here to there, then

You're living.

You're living.

Nonliving things do not breathe. They do not move on their own. They also do not reproduce. A ball of string, for example, does not create a baby ball of string!

Is it growing?

Is it growing?

Toward the sky?

Green and high?

If it needs damp ground and

Sunshine all around, then

It's a plant.
It's a plant.

Plants need more than just soil, water, and sunlight. They also need space to grow.

Is it moving?

Is it moving?

Can it fly?

Gallop by?

Animals need shelter and space in which to move around. Bigger animals usually need more space.

Living things need dinner,

Or they get much thinner.

So they need

To drink and feed.

Many animals have territories, areas where they graze or hunt for food. Big animals need lots of food. That means they need large territories.

Are you thinking?

Are you thinking?

Do you cry?

Wonder why?

Human beings are animals. We eat, drink, and sleep, like other animals. But we are also different in some ways.

People have emotions,

Thoughts and clever notions,

Feelings, too.

Yes, we do!

19

Are you living?

Are you living?

Are you not?

Are you not?

I breathe in and grow, so

Here's the fact I now know:

I'm alive!

I'm alive!

Are You Living?

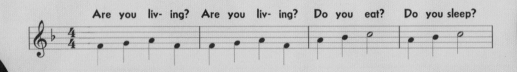

Are you liv-ing? Are you liv-ing? Do you eat? Do you sleep?

If you need to breathe air, Move from here to there, then You're liv-ing. You're liv-ing.

2. Is it growing?
Is it growing?
Toward the sky?
Green and high?
If it needs damp ground and
Sunshine all around, then
It's a plant.
It's a plant.

3. Is it moving?
Is it moving?
Can it fly?
Gallop by?
Living things need dinner,
Or they get much thinner.
So they need
To drink and feed.

4. Are you thinking?
Are you thinking?
Do you cry?
Wonder why?
People have emotions,
Thoughts and clever notions,
Feelings, too.
Yes, we do!

5. Are you living?
Are you living?
Are you not?
Are you not?
I breathe in and grow, so
Here's the fact I now know:
I'm alive!
I'm alive!

The audio file for this book is available for download at:
http://www.capstonekids.com/sciencesongs.html

Did You Know?

The word *biotic* means "living." The word *abiotic* means "nonliving."

Some animals live longer than others. The Galapagos tortoise has the longest life span on Earth. It lives an average of 200 years!

All animals eat, but some eat more often than others. A giant panda eats for about 14 hours every day. But a Burmese python is a snake that can go weeks or even months in between meals.

Plants come in all sizes. Some are huge. Sunflowers, for example, grow 8 to 12 feet (2.4 to 3.7 meters) tall. Others are tiny. More than 250 duckweed plants can fit in 1 square inch (6.5 square centimeters) of space.

Glossary

emotions—feelings; anger, happiness, and sadness are types of emotions

graze—to feed

human beings—people

reproduce—to make offspring

shelter—a safe, covered place

territory—the land on which an animal grazes or hunts for food, and raises its young

To Learn More

More Books to Read

Kalman, Bobbie. *What Is a Plant?* New York: Crabtree Pub. Co., 2000.

Ryder, Joanne. *Each Living Thing.* San Diego: Harcourt, 2000.

Salas, Laura Purdie. *Does an Elephant Fit in Your Hand? A Book About Animal Sizes.* Minneapolis: Picture Window Books, 2007.

Index

On the Web

FactHound offers a safe, fun way to find educator-approved Internet sites related to this book.

Here's what you do:

1. Visit *www.facthound.com*
2. Choose your grade level.
3. Begin your search.

This book's ID number is 9781404853027

Look for all of the books in the Science Songs series:

♪ Are You Living?
A Song About Living and Nonliving Things

♪ Home on the Earth:
A Song About Earth's Layers

♪ From Beginning to End:
A Song About Life Cycles

♪ Move It! Work It!
A Song About Simple Machines